Tipton Poetry Journal

Tipton

Tipton Poetry Journal, locat
quality poetry from Indiana a

Statistics: This issue features 35 poets from the United States (21 unique states), and 2 poets from Italy and Ukraine.

Our Featured Poem this issue is "Line in the Sand" written by Arvilla Fee. Her poem, which also receives an award of $25, can be found on page 7. The featured poem was chosen by the Board of Directors of Brick Street Poetry, Inc., the Indiana non-profit organization who publishes *Tipton Poetry Journal.*

Barry Harris reviews *The End of the Road* by Matthew Brennan

Barry Harris reviews *Left Foot, Right Foot* by Ellen Goldsmith

Cover Photo: *Zionsville Main Street* by Brendan Crowley.

Barry Harris, Editor

Copyright 2024 by the Tipton Poetry Journal.

All rights remain the exclusive property of the individual contributors and may not be used without their permission.

Tipton Poetry Journal is published by Brick Street Poetry Inc., a tax-exempt non-profit organization under IRS Code 501(c)(3). Brick Street Poetry Inc. publishes the Tipton Poetry Journal, hosts the monthly poetry series *Poetry on Brick Street* and sponsors other poetry-related events.

Tipton Poetry Journal
Contents

Charlene Langfur 1
Mary Sexson 2
Wally Swist 4
Benjamin Nash 6
Arvilla Fee 7
Mary Hills Kuck 8
Stephen R. Clark 9
Janet Butler 10
Heidi Slettedahl 10
Jim Tilley 11
Tara Menon 12
Doris Lynch 13
Tom Holmes 16
Frances Klein 17
Tia Paul-Louis 18
Gene Twaronite 20
Mykyta Ryzhykh 21
Carla Martin-Wood 22
Lynette Lamp 24
Michelle Hartman 25
John Cardwell 26
Ujjvala Bagal Rahn 27
Annette Sisson 28
Ken Meisel 30
Gil Arzola 32
Philip Athans 33
Charles Byrne 34
Margaret McGowan 34

Sam Kilkenny *36*
Jill Michelle *38*
Claire Scott *38*
Bartholomew Barker *40*
Douglas Nordfors *40*
Dana Yost *42*
Michelle Reale *43*
Bruce Levine *44*
Review: *Left Foot, Right Foot* **by Ellen Goldsmith** *45*
Review: *The End of the Road* **by Matthew Brennan** .. *49*
Contributor Biographies *52*

Tipton Poetry Journal

On the Edge of it Under a Little Moon
Charlene Langfur

I watch the tanks rolling across the TV screen and
the bombs on the A.M. news in the sky looking like stars.
This is how it is now each day in October 2023.
Afterward, I touch the green palm leaves lightly on my porch,
my fingers edging across the smooth green surface
here in the desert in the midst of winter's easy heat.
We are in a world cut loose, living with weather
we no longer expect or understand in the heat and rain.
Nothing to explain about the world, only unkindness,
most of us driving in cars when we could or should walk,
praying when we could talk to each other instead,
texting and emailing when we could take to life as it comes,
walking on the desert sands, holding hands like before,
smiling, one to one, the way we used to live more easily
when we knew exactly when to love and exactly how.

Charlene Langfur lives in Palm Springs, California, and is an LGBTQ and green writer, an organic gardener with many poems in *Poetry East, Room, Weber,* and most recently in *The Hiram Poetry Review, North Dakota Quarterly*, London's *Acumen* and an essay in the *Still Point Arts Quarterly* and a story in the *Hudson Valley Writer's Guild*.

Listening for Winter
Mary Sexson

I hear the geese
as they sail on the wide arc of sky.
They are calling the way out
so no one is left behind.

The birds from the back
seem to answer, and line
themselves up in a tighter vee
to flesh out this wide-open blue.

I want to believe
they are headed home,
to a place far south, true snowbirds
who will winter where it's warm.

But I'll stay here, as weather
tucks in around me, calls for me
to light the fire buy the tree
reach in the box for the silver star.

As the moon pulls itself into my
southern sky, gorgeous crescent that it is,
its own star set just above it
I know this is our season.

The tree warms the house, centers us,
brings us soundly down to earth,
away from any fear. We won't be left behind,
we will hear when we are called.

Tipton Poetry Journal

What I Really Needed to Know
Mary Sexson

Finding my grandfather's will
was no easy task, the glut
of paperwork I sent the clerks
trailing through, the thread
of his date of birth and proper
middle initial the thing
that got it found, and oh yeah,
I remembered the name
of his lawyer, who has also
been dead for decades, and
the year he was born, my grandfather
that is, 1890, I remembered
that too.
      How the date
was stuck in my head
is testament to my sister who
actually was the keeper
of such pertinent information
during her life, like I could go to her
for the middle name of great aunt
Inez, and end up knowing
who made the cane pole
she taught me to fish with,
more important, I think,
than knowing my grandfather's
long-dead lawyer's name, after all.

Mary Sexson lives in Indianapolis and is author of the award-winning book, *103 in the Light, Selected Poems 1996-2000 (*Restoration Press*),* and co-author of *Company of Women, New and Selected Poems* (Chatter House Press). Her poetry has appeared in *Tipton Poetry Journal, Laureate, Hoosier Lit, Flying Island, New Verse News, Grasslands Review,* and *Last Stanza Poetry Journal,* among others. She has recent work in *Reflections on Little Eagle Creek, Anti-Heroin Chic,* and *Last Stanza Poetry Journa*l Issue #8. Finishing Line Press will publish her manuscript, *Her Addiction, An Empty Place at the Table,* in 2023. Sexson's poetry is part of the INverse Poetry Archives for Hoosier Poets.

The Ear of Christ
Wally Swist

for Michael Centore

To continue to listen to what
you wrote about the ear of Christ,
that it also could be the eyes,
a foot, or even the mouth, offered
such a resonance

within me that I began
to experience what you mentioned
about the Heyschians, all of them
being eremitic, but belonging to
a larger whole,

in which their ardor
for hesychia, which is the stillness
found in quiet, rest, and silence,
and that I experienced
in my meditation today,

whereupon that emptiness
was filled with a light
in whose depths I had never
seen from afar nor had I been
in the presence of before;

and how in that I heard the rage
of my own voice in frustration
of what Tevis, who suffers from
dementia, must hear when
I seethe against her incoherence

and her memory loss, when
I release that anger towards
the grief welling up due to our
not being able to share
a simple conversation anymore.

What I also listened to, after hearing
what was monstrous in my own voice,
was the voice of the sublime,
whose sound offered the struck tone
of forgiveness, a tuning fork's hum,

that vibration ringing through me,
and in that thrum I discovered
the cleansing within me to listen
through my inner ear, and what
I heard was what Christ's ear listened to.

Wally Swist's books include *Huang Po and the Dimensions of Love* (Southern Illinois University Press, 2012), selected by Yusef Komunyakaa as co-winner in the 2011 Crab Orchard Series Open Poetry Contest, and *A Bird Who Seems to Know Me: Poems Regarding Birds & Nature* (Ex Ophidia Press, 2019), the winner of the 2018 Ex Ophidia Press Poetry Prize. His recent poems have appeared in *Asymptote, Chicago Quarterly Review, Hunger Mountain: Vermont College of Fine Arts Journal, The Montreal Review, Pensive: A Global Journal of Spirituality and the Arts, Poetry London, Scoundrel Time,* and *The Seventh Quarry Poetry Magazine (Wales).* He lives in Massachusetts.

Black Lantern
Benjamin Nash

It is a yellow light in a black lantern
in a white wooden house before
they had electricity. It is a
light in complete darkness.
A small yellow light is like
finding a good person. If only
we could shine our light like
that when bad things keep
happening to us. A light does
not seem to stop it. It is fear.

The yellow light in the black
lantern is all that is needed.
It is hope. It is the way
ahead that they talked about.
It is checking on the children
before going to bed. It is
knowing that things will work
out if we die in the night.
It is a prayer before putting
out the light. It is our dead
family that comes in the
darkness to turn on their
yellow lights and sit with us while we sleep.

Benjamin Nash lives in Austin, Texas. His poems have been published in *Louisiana Literature, 2River, Pembroke Magazine, Concho River Review,* and other publications.

Line in the Sand
Arvilla Fee

I've learned to recognize the signs:
the crossed arms, the swaying
from side to side;
it's the manic in her,
water spilling through the cracks,
the dam-about-to-break.
I've learned less is more;
some people must be loved
from a distance.
There's no cure for what ails her,
although a well-trained
psychiatrist might disagree,
heralding the virtues
of therapy and meds.
But he doesn't know her like I do—
doesn't know
about the self-medication
or the amber liquid
used to swallow pills.
He doesn't know
that she has a master's in manipulation,
or that the long shadows of her narcissism
cast blame on everyone but herself.
We're good, though—
she on her side,
me on mine.

Arvilla Fee teaches English Composition for Clark State College in Ohio and is the poetry editor for the *San Antonio Review*. She has published poetry, photography, and short stories in numerous presses, and her poetry book, *The Human Side*, is available on Amazon. For Arvilla, writing produces the greatest joy when it connects us to each other.

Sleep

Mary Hills Kuck

You're a fickle lover, seducing me
in waiting rooms, cars, churches,
libraries, then betraying me in bed.

I turn out the light, curl into position,
and you abandon me to images
of explosions, displacement,
children forced to fight,
nuclear winter, no winter,
drought, sickened water and air.

Blithely you return to tease me
with a few hours' restless dozing,
then remind me that after all,
there's more to life
than zoning out with you--

all the unmade calls,
gathering weeds, layers of dust,
unwritten poems! Can I defend
any time with you?

Eyes wide, I hear you chuckle
as you float away into dawn.

Mary Hills Kuck has spent most of her adult life in the US Northeast and in Jamaica, West Indies. Since retiring from teaching German, English, and ESOL, she has settled in Massachusetts with her husband and family. She has published poems in *The Connecticut River Review, SLANT, Tipton Poetry Journal, Burningword Literary Journal, From the Depths, Poetry Quarterly, Main St. Rag, Amethyst, The Lyric* (forthcoming) and a number of other journals. *Intermittent Sacraments,* her chapbook, was published in 2021 by Finishing Line Press. One of her poems was nominated for a Pushcart Prize.

Hello? Earth?
Stephen R. Clark

I don't think the world loves me anymore.
It used to call me up nearly every day and ask
"Hey, how're you doing?"
Now, nothing. It spins steadily beneath my feet,
shudders with a cough now and then,
but never calls. I'm not sure why.
I must have done something.
Said something. Or maybe it's because I never
really think about the earth. I never call it, never
send cards, not even on Earth Day.
Just walk on it. Trusting that it will always be there,
spinning solidly beneath my feet, holding me up
until the day it doesn't and I sink into it
and spin in silence in its embrace.

Stephen R. Clark is a writer living in Lansdale, Pennsylvaia, with his wife, BethAnn, where they attend Immanuel Church. His website is www.StephenRayClark.com. He is a member of the Evangelical Press Association and a regular contributor to the Christian Freelance Writers Network blog (tinyurl.com/cfwriters). He has published three volumes of poetry and his poems have appeared in *Christianity & Literature, Calla Press, Amethyst Review, Hoosier Lit*, and other publications. He is also a news writer for *The Baptist Paper* and contributor to the *Englewood Review of Books*. His weekly blog, "Quietly Faithful: Being a Christian Introvert," posts each Monday at ChrsitianNewsJournal.com.

Gaza
Janet Butler

An army of dark souls
plods night.
Their grief a burden
scraped away
by the cold night winds of heaven.

An army of souls
shedding earth
guided by bleak stars
on the long road to Paradise.

Janet Butler moved back to central Italy for the second time in 2018, and has remained, due in part to our turbulent political situation. She brought her adopted senior dog Rocky with her, and, in true poet fashion, a suitcase full of poetry collections and favorite watercolors. She loves Europe and Italy, but as the song says, she left her heart in San Francisco.

The Lake
Heidi Slettedahl

You don't see the colors of the lake
Until you take the photograph
Subtle shades of pink and gray
And underneath it all the swimming fish
The seaweed that tangles your ankles
The last breath of someone that you love.

Heidi Slettedahl is a US-UK dual national living in New York State who goes by a slightly different name professionally. She has been published in a variety of online literary journals and hopes to live up to her potential now that she is over 50.

The Mathematics of a Relationship
Jim Tilley

When the calculus of their relationship became
too hard to fathom, just as it had several times
earlier in the marriage, he resorted to the easier
algebra, but avoided the parabolic curves she kept
throwing at him. He looked for a straight-line
solution to their problem, tying the unknown y
to the even lesser known x. He remembered that
x + y = c, but couldn't figure out what c should
be, not much constant except the ever-present
dissension. Perhaps it was geometry he needed,
a triangle coming to mind, but knew that, too,
would soon become too complex, especially if
isosceles. In the end, he decided it'd be best if he
shrunk himself down to a point and disappeared.

Jim Tilley lives in New York State and has published three full-length collections of poetry and a novel with Red Hen Press. His short memoir, *The Elegant Solution*, was published as a Ploughshares Solo. His poem, *On the Art of Patience*, was selected by Billy Collins to win Sycamore Review's Wabash Prize for Poetry. Four of his poems have been nominated for a Pushcart Prize. His next poetry collection, *Ripples in the Fabric of the Universe: New & Selected Poems*, will be published in June 2024.

World on Canvas
Tara Menon

The sun soaks my skin,
bathing me in its buttery rays,
awakening me to my presence on earth.

I'm lucky to be alive,
to allow my senses to revel in life,
to bob my mouth under a dangling apple,
to smell the scent of flowers,
to hear the wind rush,
to recreate what I see with my brush.

I could be God
waiting for the world on my canvas to dry,
contemplating the imperfections
that allow my work to be perfect.

Tara Menon, a poet, short story writer, and essayist, has had more than seventy poems published in magazines, literary journals, and anthologies. Some of her recent poems have been published in *Cider Press Review, Last Leaves Magazine, The New Verse News,* and *The Orchards Poetry Journal.* Tara lives in Lexington, Massachusetts.

Pythagoras's Rules
Doris Lynch

My interest lies not in right triangles
nor in their celebrated diagonals as many
mistakenly assume but in mysticism and the
vagaries of diet. Imbibe no beans and no
hearts, I advised my followers.
For this and other unpopular thoughts,
my fellow citizens of Samos expelled me.
But on Crotone Island, I found Greek
students eager for new ways of thought, searching
for new philosophies. Be the first to break
into a loaf of bread, I taught them.

Their rowdy tussles at lunch made me proud.
That pride of bearded youth locked
elbow to elbow, shoving each other
away from the table. Why all this scuffling
for a round of baked wheat? Because life's
essence pours out in those first puffs
of steam. Its yeasty hymen fortifies
even eunuchs for the most arduous tasks.

Let sparrows nest in your roof,
I suggested also. To do what--create song?
Initiate music? Diogenes with the hare lip pestered.
So while you sleep, those angels will ferry
your troubles into sky. A house without
sparrows resists all beneficent dreams.

Finally, I warned my students, never,
never eat the flesh of your own dog. Not because
in doing so, you would break the caveat against eating
hearts, but because you would devour
devotion, devotion so rooted and true,
it would snuff out your life, sparrows and all.

Wandering the Sea Ice
Doris Lynch

I walked off the earth once onto the frozen
Chukchi. How many people can say that they hiked
on top of the sea? Not a wise choice. Not after reading
arctic exploration books that ended badly, or hearing
Iñupiaq stories of hunters suddenly stranded on ice islands
whisked into open water by a sudden change of current.
It wasn't smart not having a local guide—
to warn me of the textures of break-away ice,
and the vagaries of currents and wind. Not practical
either since my breasts still dribbled milk, after putting
my daughter down for a nap in the tiny
Arctic shack we shared in Kivalina that year.

I left my husband reading a battered
Elmore Leonard paperback as the old oil stove
clanked beside him. Not telling him of my plan,
because then there was no plan just the strong
pull of the ice-covered Chukchi as I walked
past Kivalina Community School. I wandered
onto the sea ice, the way you do when you're young,
and death is only a theme in a Russian novel.

That year the sea ice sang often as it carved
our shore, but that day it remained mostly silent,
offering me only a visual invitation. The ice wasn't smooth
at all but more like black land surrounded by scrabbly
pressure-ridge hills and craggy promontories.
I trudged over this hummocky world, through glistening
sculpture gardens of ice, expecting to encounter
behind each ridge a she-polar bear greedy
for my milk-scented body. I wanted to walk

forever, to Siberia, and beyond. I tried
not to think about what I'd do if the ocean
current seared the ice before or behind me,
leaving icy water in its wake. Instead I walked two miles
out toward a lead and there, only a quarter
mile away, I saw open sea water, and surrounding it,
icebergs where seals frolicked. On the upper layer of black ice
wisps of fog lifted and clouds swirled low around
this temporary plain of sea. Hundreds of winter
birds gathered, diving and rising, probably fishing
in the open lead. With great regret, I turned back
although I wanted to trek on and on.

Already, it was almost too late. In several places
I had to leap over two-foot chasms, but mostly the ice
remained intact. Several times, I turned to stare back
at the birds whirling through wisps of air as seals slid gently
into black water and steam rose into air. Although
I returned home alive, I would never trust myself
to undertake such a walk again. However, then my elation
lasted through weeks of stormy days. I can still see
seabirds swirling over the dark water, and a ringed
seal slithering, plopping off the black ice
into a sea warmer than air.

Doris Jean Lynch's poetry collection, *Swimming to Alaska,* was published by Bottom Dog Press in autumn, 2023. *Meteor Hound*, her book of haibun, also came out in 2023. In December, she was nominated for both a Pushcart Prize and a Touchstone Award for Individual Haibun. Doris lives in Bloomington, Indiana.

Lost Medieval Boy: Early Evening on Friday, August 20th, 1348
Tom Holmes

He was lifeless on the edge
of the forest. Fleas flew
from his nose and mouth.

He was beautiful.
The doctor arrived. *His belly
is warm, yet he is dead.*

His surgical knife sliced
from stomach to sternum. He pulled
from beneath the boy's lungs

a nest of baby rats living
off the heart and liver
and supping bile and blood.

They look adorable.
He threw them in the river.
It was a joy these days –

throwing and throwing up.
It meant you were healthy or just
alive. He smiled while they struggled.

He donned his mask and cloak.
*One day his belly will unfold
a remedy.* That was his prayer. I believe.

For over twenty years, **Tom Holmes** is the founding editor and curator of *Redactions: Poetry & Poetics*. Holmes is also the author of five full-length collections of poetry, including *The Book of Incurable Dr*eams (Xavier Review Press) and *The Cave*, which won The Bitter Oleander Press Library of Poetry Book Award for 2013, as well as four chapbooks. He teaches at Nashville State Community College (Clarksville). His writings about wine, poetry book reviews, and poetry can be found at his blog, The Line Break: thelinebreak.wordpress.com/. Follow him on Twitter: @TheLineBreak

Point of No Return
Frances Klein

There's no going back to the winters of childhood,
or so I'm told, though many of us seem to think
we can still take an exit we missed miles back.

Yet when my son sees snow
on a screen he makes a dove coo of wonder,
and I want so much for him to be immersed in it,
a stone tossed in the ocean, a sock lost in the covers,
something so small and engulfed it needs no name.

That snapping you hear isn't frozen branches,
it's the scaffolds of my heart when I have to break
out the microscope to see the chance
that his childhood will ever align with mine.

I watch the chasm yawning between
our parallel universes, the slow pulse like sound
waves from a bell that cannot un-ring.

I see the world his body moves through,
a new and strange planet with the audacity
to offer, with no explanation or apology,
this abundance of feeling.

Frances Klein is a poet and teacher writing at the intersection of disability and gender. She is the 2022 winner of the Robert Golden Poetry Prize, and the author of the chapbooks *New and Permanent* (Blanket Sea 2022) and *The Best Secret* (Bottlecap Press 2022). Klein lives in Ketchican, Alaska and currently serves as assistant editor of *Southern Humanities Review*. Readers can find more of her work at https://kleinpoetryblog.wordpress.com/.

Artificial Valentine
Tia Paul-Louis

I met a fellow who smiled
too often and wore a Brown
Widow tattoo on his left cheek.
He called me pretty and didn't
mind I wasn't sweet.

He'd suck a Cuban cigar
like vapor from a straw
while leaning, cross-legged,
against his Corvette, awaiting the first lean
and tipsy skinny brunette from the bar
with her top loosened. For that, I hated him.

Last night, I ripped the sleeves off
my blouse and wore my fishnets and jean
shorts with leather boots. 54-inch for
a height: I might as well have been out
of sight. He saw me as entertainingly
flawed. "I could be as tall as any woman
you'd like," I said, "if I get a lift."
So, we rode

past streetlights. Past midnight –
from cigar to syringe. My thighs
locked tighter than any cuffs and *these*

he begged to escape
like an amorous rape. And that spider tattoo
displayed an old wound of a mourning male
widow. Pleasure's where he'd find *her* – his
late beloved
again
and again.

But I was not there
to save or sympathize. *I* was no longer
safe and was now
a Brown Widow on his back
arousing a deeper sleep
than the one he lacks.

Sweet and Sour Deception
Tia Paul-Louis

2 lies and 1 cup of favor
2 tbsp honesty mixed in 12 oz of Judas kisses
1 ½ cup politics added to 1 ½ cup religion.

Pour into a shallow pan.

Let boil on medium heat
while occasionally stirring for 1 hour until thickens.

Cover and let simmer for 15 minutes, then
remove from heat.

Tia Paul-Louis is a fiction writer and poet from Florida. She began experimenting with songwriting at age 11 and later felt a deeper connection to poetry. Her themes portray family life, gender role controversies, mental health, and spiritual values. She admires the freedom of expression in most forms of art such as music, acting, and painting.

After Hearing the Young Black Poet
Gene Twaronite

After hearing the young Black poet
speak, my first reactions were
sadness, rage, then wonder
at our different worlds—
he writes of the bullet
he knows has his name on it
while I write—again—of my
imminent decrepitude,
he writes of all the times
he was stopped and frisked
while I write of indignities
suffered at airport security,
he writes of how his
great-great-great grandfather
was sold and branded like cattle
while I write of how my
Lithuanian grandfather's name
got butchered at Ellis Island,
he writes of how it felt
to watch the first black president
compared to a monkey
while I write of how
my big ears always turned red
whenever kids laughed at them,
he writes of the pain
that won't go away after
seeing his son killed because
a policeman felt threatened
while I write of the day
a policeman's wife shot her husband
dead in the bedroom above us
and I felt sad for my poor dad
cleaning bits of brain off the walls,
he writes knowing that for some
he will always be less of a man
while I write whole and secure.

Tipton Poetry Journal

We explore the separate
flows of our lives, holding
them back against time,
diving for words
in quiet pools of reflection,
but it's a wonder
his dam doesn't burst.

[This poem was first published by *Ginosko Literary Journal*]

Gene Twaronite is the author of four collections of poetry as well as the rhyming picture book *How to Eat Breakfast*. His first poetry book *Trash Picker on Mars*, published by Kelsay Books, was the winner of the 2017 New Mexico-Arizona Book Award for Arizona poetry. gene has an MA in education, and leads a poetry workshop for the University of Arizona OLLI program. A former New Englander, Gene now lives in Tucson. Follow more of his poetry at genetwaronite.poet.com

✲✲✲

Mykyta Ryzhykh

in the black box of the plane is stored the black night of the soul
we are not born on this day
we are not dead this day
we are not alive today
we are in eternal night in a dispute with God and Lucifer

[This poem was first published by *Big Windows Review*]

Mykyta Ryzhykh lives in Ukraine and is winner of the international competition Art Against Drugs and Ukrainian contests Vytoky, Shoduarivska Altanka, Khortytsky dzvony; laureate of the literary competition named after Tyutyunnik, Lyceum, Twelve, named after Dragomoshchenko. Nominated for Pushcart Prize. Published many times in the journals *Dzvin, Dnipro, Bukovinian magazine, Polutona, Rechport, Topos, Articulation, Formaslov, Literature Factory, Literary Chernihiv, Tipton Poetry Journal, Stone Poetry Journal, Divot journal, dyst journal, Superpresent Magazine, Allegro Poetry Magazine, Alternate Route, Better Than Starbucks Poetry & Fiction Journal, Littoral Press, Book of Matches*, on the portals Litcenter, *Ice Floe Press* and *Soloneba*, in the Ukrainian literary newspaper.

Words

Carla Martin-Wood

Please don't say that word –
that ugly, shriveled one
wrapped in a ball of bloody thorns
and dipped in venom.
No matter how calculated,
or how much deserved,
you don't have time to hate.
Sunsets have been teaching you that
every day of your life.

Say something else instead,
like when you were a kid
who only knew how to be honest.
You told the unfriendly neighbor,
who never gave candy on Halloween
and picked your mother's flowers,
that her dress was pretty.
She handed you an apple,
and her face lit up like sunshine.
Souls have faces, too, you know,
ask anyone.

Say something beautiful and true –
craft it like an artist.
Remember when you auditioned
for choir in tenth grade,
and the new girl who sang before you
had a voice like ripe figs and wild honey.
Before you could stop yourself,
you blurted out how lovely it was,
and she smiled shyly,
and you felt good about it,
even though you knew you'd be stuck
in back with the second sopranos
all your life.

Tipton Poetry Journal

There are plenty
croaking out a quagmire of words,
vile and dark, ten for a penny,
making all the ugly in the world,
all the wars, all the lies, all the hate,
politicians and pulpit grifters.
For you, let there be other things
while the clock is ticking down.
Let that child within you speak again.
Say to the sad clerk,
How kind you are to help me;
tell the frowning woman on the bus
What a lovely necklace you have.

Carla Martin-Wood's poems have appeared in a plethora of literary journals and anthologies since 1978, most recently, *The Orchards Poetry Journal, The Linnet's Wing,* and *The Lyric.* She lives in Birmingham, Alabama and is the author of several chapbooks, among them, *Garden of Regret* (Pudding House Publications), *Redheaded Stepchild* (Pudding House Publications) and *Absinthe & Valentines* (Flutter Press). Her work has been nominated for The Pushcart Prize several times. Her most recent full-length collection is *The Witch on Yellowhammer Hill* (The 99% Press).

Clermont Indian Hospital
Lynette Lamp

A beautiful brown girl with paint on her face
from huffing is in with kidney failure—again.
Gold gives a greater rush, the brilliant black
internist tells us. *More toluene.* More damage.
The doctor is paying back her medical education
by working here, assigns us articles on addiction.

No one from home visits the girl. We stand
in the ward, discuss acid-base balance, take notes.
I don't remember her name, but I can't forget
her eyes—beer-bottle brown, large, empty pupils.
She stares past me and the other students, knows
we have nothing new to offer. She doesn't speak, nods
permission to listen over her heart, her lungs.
Later the internist says the girl was Homecoming
Queen, a bright student—until this.

This doctor told me there was no place for her
to practice in her home state. I had no idea,
raised in a monochrome community, how she
could be left out. Except in the usual ways—
picked last for the team, no date for prom.

The brown girl in the bed stares vacantly
at the wall. She's been left out of lots of things.
There's no sparkle now. Except for the glint
of paint near her nose.

Lynette Lamp is a practicing family physician and recent graduate of the Spalding University MFA program. She has had previous poems published in *JAMA (Journal of American Medical Association), The Pharos, Annals of Internal Medicine, Dermanities, Tipton Poetry Journal*, and in *The Healing Muse,* Lynette lives in Winona, Minnesota.

Tipton Poetry Journal

Becoming silent
Michelle Hartman

When a circus disaster strikes
they send in the clowns.

I speak less these days
but my eyes note
all that transpires.

Stepping out of a race,
I never wanted to run
seeking a silent place,
work at a slow pace,
and hear myself live.

Ceasing to chase people
wrapped up in themselves,
I turn to old books
mingling with those
who built civilization
rather than
see it fall.

As the heart becomes
saturated with comfort,
intellectual challenge,
it no longer cries,
becoming content,
and learning begins.

Michelle Hartman is the author of four poetry books, four chapbooks, the most recent a winner of the John and Miriam Morris Memorial Chapbook Contest. Her work has appeared in *Crannog, Galway Review, Tipton Poetry Journal, The Atlanta Review, Penumbra, Poem, Southwestern American Review, Carve* and many more. She is the former editor of *Red River Review*, as well as the owner of Hungry Buzzard Press. Michele lives in Fort Worth, Texas.

Her Holiday
John Cardwell

She lay quiet in a nursing home bed.
Her hands and arms lying still by her sides.
A closed book was on the small table by her bed.
It looked old and fragile.
Her body breathed regularly
as her closed eyes kept looking about
for a world that would not be there
if they were open.

A son came but stayed only briefly.
Did he feel shame, fear or other emotions?
He mumbled his disjointed words
but he did manage one message:
"I love you." Then he was gone.

That was his Christmas visit.
Did she know he was there?
No one could answer that.
She lay quiet in a nursing home bed
as she had for months, not talking, eyes closed.

Once upon a time, Christmas was her favorite season.
A time of giving even though in childhood
there truly was nothing to give.
Once she received from her mom
a homemade candy made from acorns and sugar:
a gift in plain paper tied by a single ribbon.

Such was her poverty.
In later life she never threw ribbons away.
They were pressed in used books inside paper boxes.
They were her trophies of hope.
When her children committed her to a nursing home
she wailed but her protests didn't change their play.
At the facility, she cried endlessly in private moments,
though not when briefly visited, not during flickers of hope.
But in time the visits tapered away and then the silence came.
Somehow she kept a few books with her,
a few trophies of faded pinks, reds, yellows and blue.
Maybe a family member was responsible for that,
maybe a caring staff member at the institution.

After her son's visit two attendants checked on her.
The old book was next to her hand,
a pale ribbon was hanging out between the book's pages.
One staff member laid the book back on the table
and noted, "Her son must have read to her."

She lay quiet in a nursing home bed.
Christmas was her favorite season.

John Cardwell lives in Indianapolis. His latest book, *An Indiana Passage: Poems, Stories, and Essays Inspired by the Hoosier*, is a collection of poems and short stories that tell a love story about living in rural central Indiana.

Corporate: An American Sonnet
Ujjvala Bagal Rahn

I was propelled off the corporate ladder.
Thirty years of scrambling up, slipping down.
Ladder: as if we each had all the rungs
to corner suites, one for each good worker.
No: call it corporate Mount Everest,
but not Hilary and Tenzen, just one
bright figure on the Himalayan peak.
After third place VP, everyone else
is anonymous middle management -
frozen, snow-covered forgotten climbers.
Or. like me, they were kicked out of running:
too fatigued, too slow, too low on the slope
to even give a chance. No point, they said.
I left the climb behind. I did not weep.

A Pushcart nominee, **Ujjvala Rahn** was a finalist for the 2023 Loraine Williams Poetry Prize, and her second poetry collection *Memories Lounge* was a finalist for the 2021 William Faulkner – William Wisdom Creative Writing Competition. Her work has appeared in *Tipton Poetry Journal, The Threepenny Review, Illuminations, Möbius: The Journal of Social Justice* and *Bangalore Review*. She is the owner of Red Silk Press, a micropress of science fiction, science, poetry, and memoir. *Red Silk Sari* (Red Silk Press, 2013) is her first collection of poems. She lives in Savannah, Georgia.

Book of Hours
Annette Sisson

9:00

The White-Eyed Vireo's strains emerge
from the treetops, rapid chirrs spilling
into deep leaves, lake, chilly morning.

10:00

Coffee grounds coat the stainless sink
near the drain, swirl, hover, reverse—
sprayer herds them down the hole.

11:00

My husband slides the heavy glass door
in its metal track; a groundhog shambles
down the slope, round hindquarters rolling.

12:00

Uprooted trees clog the makeshift road
that snakes up the scrubby hillside where
stalks of mullein stretch into almost bloom.

1:00

On the screen an image of two airplanes, one
on its side, the other upside down—a newscaster
reciting wind speeds, marking rotations.

2:00

We wake from a haze of afternoon sleep,
your skin warm as sunlight. Breeze quavers
through screen; your mouth moves over mine.

3:00

Speckled bananas on the counter curve beside
heavy heart-shaped tomatoes tinged
green where woody stems once nestled.

4:00

The red paper wasp hovers around front-
yard basil; I pinch off the flowering
tops, drink in the leaves, peppery, citric.

5:00

The line of black clouds again opens
its maw, hail slaps the windowpane,
pearls of glass melt into restless puddles.

6:00

My daughter pulls a log from the debris, lofts it
above her head like a barbell, stows it in her hatchback—
a tiny worm inches up her bare arm.

7:00

The terrier laps her nightly allotment of water,
growls softly between tongue-strokes
as shrieking bottle rockets thunder-crack.

8:00

I touch your chest, thin muscle over bone,
sketch a trail to a forest made of limbs,
feathers, cries of heron and hawk, birdsong.

Annette Sisson's poems appear in *Valparaiso Poetry Review, Birmingham Poetry Review, Rust+Moth, Lascaux Review, Glassworks*, and many others. Her first full-length book, *Small Fish in High Branches*, was published by Glass Lyre (2022), and her second is currently questing for a publisher. Her poems have placed in *Frontier New Voices, The Fish Anthology*, and a number of other contests, and several have been nominated for The Pushcart and Best of the Net. A native Hoosier, Annette now lives in Nashville, Tennessee

City of New Orleans
Ken Meisel

Arlo's singing it, strumming it,
this ode to the American train

and we're on a front porch,
maybe in southern Illinois,

a 54' Chrysler New Yorker
hulked down under the elms,

and a 57' Ford Ranchero, red
and white, sulking by the barn,

shed roof tiles and wet white hay
spilling out of its trunk bed,

the cornfields rich all around
us and she's pulled out the wet

jar of ice tea, poured us a sip
while all around us, all along

the southbound odyssey
the train pulls out of Kankakee,

rolls along past houses, farms,
and fields. Our boy, Steve

Goodman, wrote it, strummed it
soft and brisk across the face

of an acoustic guitar so we
could drink up America like

this ice tea and vodka, but listen
to where the lyric takes us: passing

trains that have no name an'
freight yards full of old black

men and the graveyards
of the rusted automobiles ...
He's eulogizing for us the
not yet *realized*: our day breaks:

we'll be gone 500 miles
when the day is done.

Ken Meisel is a poet and psychotherapist, a 2012 Kresge Arts Literary Fellow, a Pushcart Prize nominee and the author of eight books of poetry. His most recent books are: *Our Common Souls: New & Selected Poems of Detroit* (Blue Horse Press: 2020) and *Mortal Lullabies* (FutureCycle Press: 2018). Meisel has recent work in *Concho River Review, I-70 Review, San Pedro River Review,* and *Rabid Oak*. Ken lives in Dearborn, Michigan.

The Accident On Highway 30
Gil Arzola

what were the last words she said to you?
she must have noticed
      two blackbirds fly into the ditch bank just
before she turned onto the highway to die,
she must have seen
      corn fields dancing in the July breeze.

everything becomes a distraction eventually.

      she left some dishes soaking and
      you were annoyed a little.
the yolk of half eaten eggs running as slowly
down the drain
as warm blood on pavement.

she was in a hurry is all.
we all hurry. but
what was the last thing
she said to you? do you remember?

the last thing she thought that mattered
before she went
out the door to die?

Gil Arzola is the second son of a former migrant worker living with his wife in Valparaiso, Indiana. Winner of the 2019 Passager Poetry Contest and the 2021 Rattle Poetry Chapbook Contest, he has been nominated for two Pushcart Awards. His book of poetry, *Prayers of Little Consequence* was published in 2019 and a chapbook, *The Death of a Migrant Worker*, was published in 2021. His work has appeared in *Crosslimb, The Elysian Review, The Notre Dame Review, Palabra, The Tipton Poetry Journal, Craft, Acentos Review* and *Rattle* among others.

Tipton Poetry Journal

A House of Broken Things
Philip Athans

He lived in a house full of broken things
They didn't used to be broken
But along the way they broke
Sometimes he fixed them
Sometimes he bought new things
But sometimes things stayed broken
Even though he didn't want them
To stay broken
But there were so many things
And he was so tired
And the more things broke
And the more expensive things got
The more tired he became
Until, finally
He lived in a house of broken things
And at first he hated it
He wanted to fix it
Then wanted to sell it
To burn it all down
Then he finally just
Lived
In his house of things that were as broken as he was
And it wasn't that bad
It was fine

He was fine.

Editor and author **Philip Athans** has been a driving force behind varied media including *Alternative fiction & poetry* magazine and Wizards of the Coast. He lives and works in the Pacific Northwest.

The problem of induction
Charles Byrne

Tomorrow
is another day.

The sun has risen
every morning

and set every evening,
so far as we know,

so far.

Charles Byrne is a writer living now in Brooklyn, New York, with other poems recently published or forthcoming in *Meridian, Notre Dame Review* and *Sonora Review*.

Pileated Woodpecker
Margaret McGowan

I've only seen
one in my lifetime

On a walk
in the back country
I came across
an ancient chamber
undamaged by progress,
the staggering scent of decay
and renewal, a canopy
that nearly blotted out
the sky, no trail, just the path
that I could construct
on the woodland floor.

It was perched on the branch
of a fat maple. Its plump body
the length of a staff. A crimson tuft
crowned its primitive head. A black cape
hung flawlessly over its white evening shirt.

I froze, my mouth agape,
watched as it hurriedly flew off,
its body too bulky to glide
like a sparrow. Instead it moved
with deliberate elegance
and poise.

It must have heard
the forest's crackling noises,
the debris under my feet,
the rotting things of the woods:
desiccated branches, twigs, and leaves.

It must have known
a being not belonging
had entered its kingdom.

Margaret McGowan has a BA in English Education from UAlbany, State University of New York and is the author of *Ancestors and Other Poems* (2021). She was a finalist in the 2022 Stephen A. DiBiase Poetry Contest and received an Honorable Mention in the HVWG Poetry Contest 2019. Her poems have been published in *Qu, Hobart, Moon Park Review, The Raven Review, Eunoia Review*, and elsewhere.

The Aftermath
Sam Kilkenny

The sun still rises,
Though they torched the fields yesterday,
Turned our houses into barracks.
And we still rise,
Though we're not in our beds any longer,
Though we don't know what to do,
We don't know where to go.

Sam Kilkenny is a nonfiction writer and poet. He lives in Atlanta, Georgia, where he writes everyday. He is currently writing with C.W. Bryan at poetryispretentious.com. His work can be found on the website, most notably his poems for the *Poetry is Plagiarism* Series.

Neighbors
William Heath

The guy with the Walt Whitman beard
lives down the valley in a clapboard
colonial house so close to the road
you can judge its age. One evening
he shows up at my front door, wants
to talk. I have only a few neighbors
yet I don't ask him in.

As we stand on my fieldstone porch
I note his bicycle tipped on its side,
wire handlebar basket brimming over
with quart bottles of cheap beer.
I often see him pedaling into town
two miles away to replenish his stash.
His ruby face betrays he's far gone
before he spills out his slurred words.

NASA has rejected three-hundred-
and-sixty-seven of his inventions because
it has been taken over by Venusians
from outer space. I nod and ask how
he knows who they are. They have
a strange look about them, their heads
aren't on straight.

Weeks later, wandering in woods
that frame this valley located between
Esopus and New Paltz, close to
the Hudson River, I come upon him
crouched by a small waterfall
rearranging stones, he looks up
and says, "I think Nature should look
as neat as possible, don't you?"

This gentleness is belied each weekend
when his mother brings food and clothes,
hauls off the laundry. Their fierce arguments
last hours, bloodcurdling screams echo
in the valley. I feel certain he'll strangle her,
yet the following day he's out puttering in
his yard, the next weekend his mother
drives up with fresh supplies.

William Heath lives in Maryland and has published two books of poems, *The Walking Man* and *Steel Valley Elegy*; two chapbooks, *Night Moves in Ohio* and *Leaving Seville*; three novels: *The Children Bob Moses Led* (winner of the Hackney Award), *Devil Dancer*, and *Blacksnake's Path*; a work of history, *William Wells and the Struggle for the Old Northwest* (winner of two Spur Awards); and a collection of interviews, *Conversations with Robert Stone*. www.williamheathbooks.com

Alzheimer's Accessories
Jill Michelle

after Aleksandr Blok

Cellphone, keys, wallet, hat—
things we'd have to find before
Friday lunch dates in the years that
tracked his decline from father

back to child, who can't go alone
to the restroom, needs you to read
the menu, remember the way home,
remind him to grab his hat and keys.

Jill Michelle's latest poems appear/are forthcoming in *Hawai`i Pacific Review, LEON Literary Review, New Ohio review, Red Flag Poetry,* and *Drunk Monkeys*. Her poem, "On Our Way Home," won the 2023 NORward Prize for Poetry. She teaches at Valencia College in Orlando, Florida. Find more of her work at byjillmichelle.com.

My Neighbor's Father Died
Claire Scott

Her hair, normally pure perfection,
is frowzy with split ends. her glitter-green
nails chipped and gnawed. black eyes stare
from the bottom of a well. she wears
shabby sweats and soiled slippers
to the grocery store, returning
with an empty bag draped over
a pencil-thin arm. I notice the plants
on her porch are turning brown,
newspapers piling up.

And I am jealous.
when my father died
I went to his dry-eyed funeral.
my life didn't stop, hay foot, straw foot.
I didn't reminisce
about all the good times with my father
who was distant, his days dictated by the clock,
dinner at seven, bed at ten. no raucous
tickling or cheating at Crazy Eights.
no snowmen with carrot ears and raisin noses
She saw her father every day at the end
held his hand, fed him sherbet. she showed
me some old pictures. In one he is wearing
a Luke Skywalker mask while she is
dressed as a delighted Yoda.
here's one at her fifth birthday, blowing
candles, needing a little help,
and another with him reading *Frog and Toad*.
I cried for the first time
for the father I didn't have.

Claire Scott is an award winning poet in Oakland, California who has received multiple Pushcart Prize nominations. Her work has been accepted by the *Atlanta Review, Bellevue Literary Review, New Ohio Review, Enizagam* and *Healing Muse* among others. Claire is the author of *Waiting to be Called* and *Until I Couldn't*. She is the co-author of Unfolding in Light: A Sisters' Journey in Photography and Poetry.

Eclipse
Bartholomew Barker

When darkness struck, I shivered
even though I knew exactly
when it would happen and why,
visiting my daughter's grave
for the first time.

The eclipse wasn't my fault
unlike her death and the divorce.
I had no memory of the accident.
I trusted the investigators
but my guilt was intellectual
unlike that visceral fear
in the pit of my stomach
as the umbra crossed the Earth.

I wouldn't run into her mother
that afternoon at the cemetery
resting in the path of totality.
There were others around
but just for the astronomy.

I was the one looking down.

[This poem was first published by *Sledgehammer Lit*]

Bartholomew Barker is one of the organizers of Living Poetry, a collection of poets and poetry lovers in the Triangle region of North Carolina. His first poetry collection, *Wednesday Night Regular*, written in and about strip clubs, was published in 2013. His second, *Milkshakes and Chilidogs*, a chapbook of food inspired poetry was served in 2017. He was nominated for a Pushcart Prize in 2021. Born and raised in Ohio, studied in Chicago, he worked in Connecticut for nearly twenty years before moving to Hillsborough, North Carolina, where he makes money as a computer programmer to fund his poetry habit.

A Mortal Man
Douglas Nordfors

She cries

out to him to come out and see the lettuce heads—
they've grown bigger than they were!

Instead,

he drops the side of his face onto a pillow
that has never hurt or spared him.
His bed,

anchored to the ceiling and the stars, is far and away
the last thing that can help him wake up
from dread

of life before death. What he will do after death
no one will know. His knees don't raise their voices.
Rhyme doesn't rhyme.

Heads have no faces. One voice raised
an impossibility. The fetal position won't draw his knees
down, or paint a picture of his birth, and life

before death (that phrase again), as immediate
as it is, isn't
right there to comfort him. Still, one side of him

rolls out of bed, and dread
puts on the clothes that make him stand up
to the ceiling and the sun, and go out

and see with the eyes embedded in his head
her voice in a soft voice now
telling him, in so many words,

to stop
giving himself the last word
that follows after "after."

Douglas Nordfors, a native of Seattle, now lives in Virginia. He has a BA from Columbia University and an MFA in poetry from The University of Virginia. Poems have been published in journals as *The Iowa Review, Quarterly West, Poetry Northwest, Poet Lore, Louisville Review, Charlton Review, Potomac Review, California Quarterly, Evansville Review, The Hampden-Sydney Poetry Review, Valparaiso Poetry Review* and others. His three books of poetry are *Auras* (2008), *The Fate Motif* (2013), and *Half-Dreaming* (2020), all published by Plain View Press.

Copy-editing on Deadline
Dana Yost

Deadline in 10 minutes
and this story is late.
yet it has to go in. Tonight.
I swear out loud. Yes I do that.
Especially on deadline.
But the story is clean.
The lede works. The second
graf explains what happened
--school board voted to fire
a superintendent. Not for
anything serious. Personality
conflicts, is what the board
chairman says. Lawrence,
our lead pressman, is standing
behind me. Not that he says
anything. But I can feel it.
Years of this stuff, and you
know when Lawrence is behind
You. Yes, yes, it's coming.
I fix a typo late in the story,
Then put it on the page
and send the whole page
straight to plate. Modern
technology, eh? Costs money
but saves time. If I smoked,
I'd step outside and light up
now. But I don't, so I don't.
My heart is still on dirt-track
racer mode. Flying. Deadline
does that. I have lived for it
all my adult life. I wad a sheet
of paper, aim for a trash can.
Bucket. Dead-on. Ha, I say.
Try beating me tonight.

Since 2008, **Dana Yost** has published eight books with a ninth forthcoming from Finishing Line Press and has been nominated for three Pushcart Prizes and won the 2020 chapbook contest of the South Dakota State Poetry Society. Dana lives in Sioux Falls, South Dakota.

Elemental

Michelle Reale

On the avenue, ghost signs blush on repurposed brick buildings. People
are leaving us. It was bound to happen. Nothing can anchor them here anymore,
not their cigarettes, mortgages, love affairs, imminent deadlines , unsaid
 proclamations of love, or their freshly stocked pantries.

There are hollow spaces where they used to be,
silk dopamine threads of being, left behind. Molecules of their breath hang
in spaces that have outlived them, and will outlive us.
Decay is marked by successive decades,

and the satin lined coffin is an aura that haunts our days.
But the ones who are leaving,
and the ones who have left , leave their imprint like a shadow on an x-ray.
I see them, I walk through them. They fidget in their somber clothes.

Their sorrow is latent. They pass on the fear of what they have endured.
We are porous and so we understand and receive what they give.
There are phases to everything and if we look close enough
we see that the beginning contains the end, as well.

The new moon is elemental, as always.
Our desires continue to beg for the care and attention
we are too distracted to give. Time plays itself out
then is gone without even a glance in our direction.

Michelle Reale is the author of several poetry collections, her most recent *In the Year of Hurricane Agnes* (Alien Buddha Press, 2023) and *Confini: Poems of Refugees in Sicily* (Červená Barva Press, 2022). She is the Founding and Managing Editor of OVUNQUE SIAMO: NEW ITALIAN-AMERICAN WRITING and she teaches poetry in Arcadia University's low-residency MFA program in Glenside, Pennsylvania.

Tipton Poetry Journal
The World Goes Forward
Bruce Levine

The world goes forward
For better or worse
Time travels at the speed of light
Toward its own destiny
Artists toil under the canopy
  of forgotten memories
In the age of technology
Does anyone care
We surround ourselves
In a glass bubble
  of our own making
Shielding the sun's rays
  from reality
While bending them into conformity
The bubble bursts
And time is thrown into the vortex
Screaming for surrender
A temper-tantrum of fate
Grasping at straws
Yet knowing no relief
Forever the moment
Held in a wine glass
  of shimmering incandescence
As the world goes forward
Without relief

Bruce Levine has spent his life as a writer of fiction and poetry and as a music and theatre professional. A 2019 *Pushcart Prize* Poetry nominee, a 2021 *Spillwords Press Awards* winner, the *Featured Writer* in WestWard Quarterly Summer 2021 and his bio is featured in *"Who's Who of Emerging Writers 2020."* Bruce has over three hundred works published on over twenty-five on-line journals including *Ariel Chart, Spillwords, The Drabble*; in over seventy print books including *Poetry Quarterly, Haiku Journal, Tipton Poetry Journal; Halcyon Days Founder's Favourites* (on-line and print) and his shows have been produced in New York and around the country. His work is dedicated to the loving memory of his late wife, Lydia Franklin. A native Manhattanite, Bruce now lives and writes in Maine. Visit him at www.brucelevine.com

Review: *Left Foot, Right Foot* by Ellen Goldsmith
Reviewed by Barry Harris

Title: Left Foot, Right Foot

Author: Ellen Goldsmith

Year: 2021

Publisher: Maine Authors Publishing

Left Foot, Right Foot by Ellen Goldsmith is a collection that explores illness, recovery, and the beauty of everyday life. The poems offer an honest reflection on the human experience. Goldsmith's writing is both lyrical and accessible, with an eye for detail and a gift for capturing the essence of a moment. Her descriptions of nature are vivid, evoking a sense of wonder and awe at the world around us. The poems draw on the author's own experiences of illness and recovery which lends the collection a sense of authenticity and emotional depth, as Goldsmith explores the challenges of facing a diagnosis, the process of healing, and the importance of resilience and perseverance.

The title is significant in relation to the poems in this collection as it serves as a mantra of recovery. The phrase is a simple reminder to keep moving forward, one step at a time, even in times of adversity. It represents the journey of recovery and the importance of perseverance, as well as the idea that progress can be made through small, incremental steps. The phrase "Left Foot, Right Foot" serves as a powerful symbol of the journey of recovery, both physical and emotional, and the importance of taking things one step at a time.

Goldsmith's rare and life-threatening illness took place during the COVID pandemic. Her poem simply titled "Covid," reflects on the impact of the pandemic. The poem captures a dreamlike quality depicting a scene where hospital staff are having breakfast on a hill before tending to the sick. The poem conveys a sense of longing for connection and normalcy during a time of uncertainty.

> *The same dream over and over.*
> *The hospital staff is having breakfast on a hill.*
> *Their colorful blankets and fancy baskets*
> *almost cover the grass. Seated in groups,*
> *they call to each other, shouting, laughing—*
> *doctors, nurses, administrators, orderlies.*
> *I'm so happy that in the drab days*
> *of COVID, before they tend the sick,*
> *they have morning fun! I want to ask*
> *my nurses what they brought to the picnic.*

The author utilizes the ordinary, daily events of her day to tell the story of her personal journey. In "Another Country," she explains to us:

> *Every room in my house is a waiting room,*
> *whether I read a book, bake a cake,*
> *watch TV, or Windex our glass tables,*
> *what I'm really doing is waiting.*

And in "Rosemary Chicken," Goldsmith centers her emotions during food preparation:

> *I want to peel*
> *two heads of garlic,*
> *maybe more.*
> *I want to sauté*
> *the pieces of chicken*
> *to perfection,*
> *cook down the wine,*
> *add the rosemary,*
> *breathe in*
> *the intensifying aromas.*
>
> *I want to be in the pause*
> *between preparation*
> *and feasting.*

In the book's final poem, "I No Longer Have a Favorite Color," Goldsmith leaves us with this thought:

> *Almost dying removes preferences.*
> *What's better about grass*
> *than a layer of fallen leaves?*

Left Foot, Right Foot is a moving collection of poems that reflects on the human experience. Goldsmith's writing is both beautiful and honest, and captures the complexity and beauty of life. This is a collection that will resonate with readers on a deep and personal level, offering comfort, inspiration, and a reminder of the power of the human spirit.

Ellen Goldsmith is a poet and teacher. Her books include *Left Foot, Right Foot, Where to Look, Such Distances* and *No Pine Tree in This Forest Is Perfect*, which won the 1997 Slapering Hol Press Chapbook Competition and was described by Dennis Nurkse as an "incandescent collection." Her poems have appeared in many journals and in anthologies.

She earned an Ed.D. from Teachers College, Columbia University, has an M.A. in English from City College and graduated Phi Beta Kappa from Queens College. She is Professor Emeritus from the City University of New York. In 2006, she relocated to Maine, where she enjoys the rich literary landscape of the Midcoast as well as the always changing views of Broad Cove from her home in Cushing. For her, poetry is essential, a way to explore and discover, uncover and recover.

Barry Harris is editor of the *Tipton Poetry Journal* and several anthologies by Brick Street Poetry. He has published one poetry collection, *Something At The Center*. Married and father of two grown sons, Barry lives in Brownsburg, Indiana and is retired from Eli Lilly and Company.

His poetry has appeared in *Kentucky Review, Valparaiso Poetry Review, Grey Sparrow, Silk Road Review, Saint Ann's Review, North Dakota Quarterly, Boston Literary Magazine, Night Train, Silver Birch Press, Flying Island, Awaken Consciousness, Writers' Bloc, Red-Headed Stepchild* and *Laureate: The Literary Journal of Arts for Lawrence*.

He graduated a long time ago with a major in English from Ball State University.

Tipton Poetry Journal

Review: *The End of the Road* by Matthew Brennan

Reviewed by Barry Harris

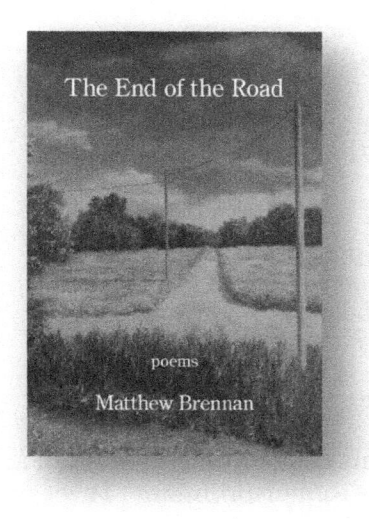

Title: *The End of the Road*

Author: Matthew Brennan

Year: 2023

Publisher: Kelsay Books

Matthew Brennan's seventh book of poetry, *The End of the Road*, points toward the end of a road. But the author begins the book with stories, memories and reflections on the beginning of the road that his life took beginning in St. Louis, then at college at Grinnell College in Iowa and the University of Minnesota, before moving to the streets of Terre Haute, Indiana where he taught poetry and literature for 32 years at Indiana State University.

Brennan has included several persona poems where he grants poetic voice to his subjects such as Joseph Haydn in "Haydn Unbound;" the characters Emma and Charles from Madame Bovary in "Emma at the Opera;" Madame Edith Brown (a nineteenth century madame of Terre Haute's notorious red light district) in "Madame Edith Brown, Proprietor;" Hoosier writer Theodoroe Dreiser (relating his letter to Eugene Debs, imprisoned for sedition at the Atlanta Federal Penetentiary) in the eponymous "Theodore Dreiser;" and a baseball tribute to Terre Haute area pitcher, Mordecai Brown in "Mordecai Three Finger Brown."

Brennan has a knack for focusing on ordinary scenes from his life and gracing his readers with emotional lessons he then shares gladly. In "Fool for Love: Belated Recognition," he paints a scene from his youth where he waits in a Des Moines bus station:

49

> I dreamed the bus would wheel me away
> from dead-ends like this joint, but when the jukebox
> boomed "Oh, Lonesome Me," I looked into
> the mirror by the bar, surprised to find
>
> the face that met my stupid gaze was mine.

There are no fewer than three poems dedicated to his wife, Beverley. In a tender remembrance, *Valentine's Day, Thirty Years Ago*, Brennan relates how he:

> . . . tried but could not read your mind, though now
> In hindsight what I best remember is
> Your Mona Lisa smile and bold blue eyes
> Taking in my full measure, knowing what
> I would not know till dawn, the slightest light
> Around us, loose but binding, like a kiss.

There are several ekphrastic poems in this collection; two of them address the paintings by Brennan's brother, Christopher Brennan: "Three Windows in an Empty Room," and the title and cover illustration, "The End of the Road." Taking a brief artistic detour from Brennan's poetry to his brother's paintings of urban landscapes is a side trip worth taking. You can see more at http://christopherbrennan.net/.

The final (and also title) poem, "The End of the Road," seems to summarize this look back at a life lived:

> Now that I'm here, it went so fast:
> The bright suburban cul-de-sacs
> Of youth, the lanes where time once stalled.
> And then the teeming beltway traffic,
> Long drives between the trucks on mountain
> Passes that opened in the fog
> To views I'd never seen, not even
> When I counted fifty years.
> . . . One last stop —
> Then up ahead, beneath a bank
> Of blackening clouds, a dark wood
> I almost recognize, waiting
> to greet my late arrival.

Tipton Poetry Journal

You might like to take a quick look at the book cover to glimpse the blackening clouds and dark woods Brennan sees waiting at the end of a long and fulfilled road.

Matthew Brennan is the author of seven books of poetry and four of criticism. He has published poems and articles in many journals, including *Poetry Ireland Review, Sewanee Review* and *The New York Times Book Review*. His many honors include the Theodore Dreiser Distinguished Research and Creativity Award and the Thomas Merton Center Prize for Poetry of the Sacred. His 2009 poetry collection, *The House with the Mansard Roof*, was a finalist for Best Books of Indiana. He formerly taught poetry writing and Romanticism at Indiana State University. He resides in Columbus, Ohio.

Barry Harris is editor of the *Tipton Poetry Journal* and several anthologies by Brick Street Poetry. He has published one poetry collection, *Something At The Center*. Married and father of two grown sons, Barry lives in Brownsburg, Indiana and is retired from Eli Lilly and Company.

His poetry has appeared in *Kentucky Review, Valparaiso Poetry Review, Grey Sparrow, Silk Road Review, Saint Ann's Review, North Dakota Quarterly, Boston Literary Magazine, Night Train, Silver Birch Press, Flying Island, Awaken Consciousness, Writers' Bloc, Red-Headed Stepchild* and *Laureate: The Literary Journal of Arts for Lawrence*.

He graduated a long time ago with a major in English from Ball State University.

Tipton Poetry Journal

Contributor Biographies

Gil Arzola is the second son of a former migrant worker living with his wife in Valparaiso, Indiana. Winner of the 2019 Passager Poetry Contest and the 2021 Rattle Poetry Chapbook Contest, he has been nominated for two Pushcart Awards. His book of poetry, *Prayers of Little Consequence* was published in 2019 and a chapbook, *The Death of a Migrant Work*er, was published in 2021. His work has appeared in *Crosslimb, The Elysian Review, The Notre Dame Review, Palabra, The Tipton Poetry Journal, Craft, Acentos Review* and *Rattle* among others.

Editor and author **Philip Athans** has been a driving force behind varied media including *Alternative fiction & poetry* magazine and Wizards of the Coast. He lives and works in the Pacific Northwest.

Bartholomew Barker is one of the organizers of Living Poetry, a collection of poets and poetry lovers in the Triangle region of North Carolina. His first poetry collection, *Wednesday Night Regular*, written in and about strip clubs, was published in 2013. His second, *Milkshakes and Chilidogs*, a chapbook of food inspired poetry was served in 2017. He was nominated for a Pushcart Prize in 2021. Born and raised in Ohio, studied in Chicago, he worked in Connecticut for nearly twenty years before moving to Hillsborough, North Carolina, where he makes money as a computer programmer to fund his poetry habit.

Janet Butler moved back to central Italy for the second time in 2018, and has remained, due in part to our turbulent political situation. She brought her adopted senior dog Rocky with her, and, in true poet fashion, a suitcase full of poetry collections and favorite watercolors. She loves Europe and Italy, but as the song says, she left her heart in San Francisco.

Charles Byrne is a writer living now in Brooklyn, New York, with other poems recently published or forthcoming in *Meridian, Notre Dame Review* and *Sonora Review*.

John Cardwell lives in Indianapolis. His latest book, *An Indiana Passage: Poems, Stories, and Essays Inspired by the Hoosier*, is a collection of poems and short stories that tell a love story about living in rural central Indiana.

Stephen R. Clark is a writer living in Lansdale, Pennsylvaia, with his wife, BethAnn, where they attend Immanuel Church. His website is www.StephenRayClark.com. He is a member of the Evangelical Press Association and a regular contributor to the Christian Freelance Writers Network blog (tinyurl.com/cfwriters). He has published three volumes of poetry and his poems have appeared in *Christianity & Literature, Calla Press, Amethyst Review, Hoosier Lit*, and other publications. He is also a news writer for *The Baptist Paper* and contributor to the *Englewood Review of Books*. His weekly blog, "Quietly Faithful: Being a Christian Introvert," posts each Monday at ChrsitianNewsJournal.com.

After 34 years with Eli Lilly and Company, **Brendan Crowley** set up his own consulting and executive coaching business, Brendan Crowley Advisors LLC. He helps executives grow in their roles and careers. Brendan is originally from Ireland and lives with his wife Rosaleen in Zionsville, Indiana. He has a passion for photography and loves taking photographs of his home country, Ireland, and here in Indiana.

Arvilla Fee teaches English Composition for Clark State College in Ohio and is the poetry editor for the *San Antonio Review*. She has published poetry, photography, and short stories in numerous presses, and her poetry book, *The Human Side*, is available on Amazon. For Arvilla, writing produces the greatest joy when it connects us to each other.

Michelle Hartman is the author of four poetry books, four chapbooks, the most recent a winner of the John and Miriam Morris Memorial Chapbook Contest. Her work has appeared in *Crannog, Galway Review, Tipton Poetry Journal, The Atlanta Review, Penumbra, Poem, Southwestern American Review, Carve* and many more. She is the former editor of *Red River Review*, as well as the owner of Hungry Buzzard Press. Michele lives in Fort Worth, Texas.

William Heath lives in Maryland and has published two books of poems, *The Walking Man* and *Steel Valley Elegy*; two chapbooks, *Night Moves in Ohio* and *Leaving Seville*; three novels: *The Children Bob Moses Led* (winner of the Hackney Award), *Devil Dancer*, and *Blacksnake's Path*; a work of history, *William Wells and the Struggle for the Old Northwest* (winner of two Spur Awards); and a collection of interviews, *Conversations with Robert Stone*. www.williamheathbooks.com

For over twenty years, **Tom Holmes** is the founding editor and curator of *Redactions: Poetry & Poetics*. Holmes is also the author of five full-length collections of poetry, including *The Book of Incurable Dr*eams (Xavier Review Press) and *The Cave*, which won The Bitter Oleander Press Library of Poetry Book Award for 2013, as well as four chapbooks. He teaches at Nashville State Community College (Clarksville). His writings about wine, poetry book reviews, and poetry can be found at his blog, The Line Break: thelinebreak.wordpress.com/. Follow him on Twitter: @TheLineBreak

Sam Kilkenny is a nonfiction writer and poet. He lives in Atlanta, Georgia, where he writes everyday. He is currently writing with C.W. Bryan at poetryispretentious.com. His work can be found on the website, most notably his poems for the *Poetry is Plagiarism* Series.

Frances Klein is a poet and teacher writing at the intersection of disability and gender. She is the 2022 winner of the Robert Golden Poetry Prize, and the author of the chapbooks *New and Permanent* (Blanket Sea 2022) and *The Best Secret* (Bottlecap Press 2022). Klein lives in Ketchikan, Alaska and currently serves as assistant editor of *Southern Humanities Review*. Readers can find more of her work at https://kleinpoetryblog.wordpress.com/.

Mary Hills Kuck has spent most of her adult life in the US Northeast and in Jamaica, West Indies. Since retiring from teaching German, English, and ESOL, she has settled in Massachusetts with her husband and family. She has published poems in *The Connecticut River Review, SLANT, Tipton Poetry Journal, Burningword Literary Journal, From the Depths, Poetry Quarterly, Main St. Rag, Amethyst, The Lyric* (forthcoming) and a number of other journals. *Intermittent Sacraments*, her chapbook, was published in 2021 by Finishing Line Press. One of her poems was nominated for a Pushcart Prize.

Tipton Poetry Journal

Lynette Lamp is a practicing family physician and recent graduate of the Spalding University MFA program. She has had previous poems published in *JAMA (Journal of American Medical Association), The Pharos, Annals of Internal Medicine, Dermanities, Tipton Poetry Journal,* and in *The Healing Muse,* Lynette lives in Winona, Minnesota.

Charlene Langfur lives in Palm Springs, California, and is an LGBTQ and green writer, an organic gardener with many poems in *Poetry East, Room, Weber,* and most recently in *The Hiram Poetry Review, North Dakota Quarterly,* London's *Acumen* and an essay in the *Still Point Arts Quarterly* and a story in the *Hudson Valley Writer's Guild.*

Bruce Levine has spent his life as a writer of fiction and poetry and as a music and theatre professional. A 2019 *Pushcart Prize* Poetry nominee, a 2021 *Spillwords Press Awards* winner, the *Featured Writer* in WestWard Quarterly Summer 2021 and his bio is featured in *"Who's Who of Emerging Writers 2020."* Bruce has over three hundred works published on over twenty-five on-line journals including *Ariel Chart, Spillwords, The Drabble*; in over seventy print books including *Poetry Quarterly, Haiku Journal, Tipton Poetry Journal; Halcyon Days Founder's Favourites* (on-line and print) and his shows have been produced in New York and around the country. His work is dedicated to the loving memory of his late wife, Lydia Franklin. A native Manhattanite, Bruce now lives and writes in Maine. Visit him at www.brucelevine.com

Doris Jean Lynch's poetry collection, *Swimming to Alaska,* was published by Bottom Dog Press in autumn, 2023. *Meteor Hound,* her book of haibun, also came out in 2023. In December, she was nominated for both a Pushcart Prize and a Touchstone Award for Individual Haibun. Doris lives in Bloomington, Indiana.

Carla Martin-Wood's poems have appeared in a plethora of literary journals and anthologies since 1978, most recently, *The Orchards Poetry Journal, The Linnet's Wing,* and *The Lyric.* She lives in Birmingham, Alabama and is the author of several chapbooks, among them, *Garden of Regret* (Pudding House Publications), *Redheaded Stepchild* (Pudding House Publications) and *Absinthe & Valentines* (Flutter Press). Her work has been nominated for The Pushcart Prize several times. Her most recent full-length collection is *The Witch on Yellowhammer Hill* (The 99% Press).

Margaret McGowan has a BA in English Education from UAlbany, State University of New York and is the author of *Ancestors and Other Poems* (2021). She was a finalist in the 2022 Stephen A. DiBiase Poetry Contest and received an Honorable Mention in the HVWG Poetry Contest 2019. Her poems have been published in *Qu, Hobart, Moon Park Review, The Raven Review, Eunoia Review,* and elsewhere.

Ken Meisel is a poet and psychotherapist, a 2012 Kresge Arts Literary Fellow, a Pushcart Prize nominee and the author of eight books of poetry. His most recent books are: *Our Common Souls: New & Selected Poems of Detroit* (Blue Horse Press: 2020) and *Mortal Lullabies* (FutureCycle Press: 2018). Meisel has recent work in *Concho River Review, I-70 Review, San Pedro River Review,* and *Rabid Oak.* Ken lives in Dearborn, Michigan.

Tara Menon, a poet, short story writer, and essayist, has had more than seventy poems published in magazines, literary journals, and anthologies. Some of her recent poems have been published in *Cider Press Review, Last Leaves Magazine, The New Verse News,* and *The Orchards Poetry Journal.* Tara lives in Lexington, Massachusetts.

Tipton Poetry Journal

Jill Michelle's latest poems appear/are forthcoming in *Hawai`i Pacific Review, LEON Literary Review, New Ohio review, Red Flag Poetry,* and *Drunk Monkeys*. Her poem, "On Our Way Home," won the 2023 NORward Prize for Poetry. She teaches at Valencia College in Orlando, Florida. Find more of her work at byjillmichelle.com.

Benjamin Nash lives in Austin, Texas. His poems have been published in *Louisiana Literature, 2River, Pembroke Magazine, Concho River Review,* and other publications.

Douglas Nordfors, a native of Seattle, now lives in Virginia. He has a BA from Columbia University and an MFA in poetry from The University of Virginia. Poems have been published in journals as *The Iowa Review, Quarterly West, Poetry Northwest, Poet Lore, Louisville Review, Charlton Review, Potomac Review, California Quarterly, Evansville Review, The Hampden-Sydney Poetry Review, Valparaiso Poetry Review* and others. His three books of poetry are *Auras* (2008), *The Fate Motif* (2013), and *Half-Dreaming* (2020), all published by Plain View Press.

Tia Paul-Louis is a fiction writer and poet from Florida. She began experimenting with songwriting at age 11 and later felt a deeper connection to poetry. Her themes portray family life, gender role controversies, mental health, and spiritual values. She admires the freedom of expression in most forms of art such as music, acting, and painting.

A Pushcart nominee, **Ujjvala Rahn** was a finalist for the 2023 Loraine Williams Poetry Prize, and her second poetry collection *Memories Lounge* was a finalist for the 2021 William Faulkner – William Wisdom Creative Writing Competition. Her work has appeared in *Tipton Poetry Journal, The Threepenny Review, Illuminations, Möbius: The Journal of Social Justice* and *Bangalore Review*. She is the owner of Red Silk Press, a micropress of science fiction, science, poetry, and memoir. *Red Silk Sari* (Red Silk Press, 2013) is her first collection of poems. She lives in Savannah, Georgia.

Michelle Reale is the author of several poetry collections, her most recent *In the Year of Hurricane Agnes* (Alien Buddha Press, 2023) and *Confini: Poems of Refugees in Sicily* (Červená Barva Press, 2022). She is the Founding and Managing Editor of OVUNQUE SIAMO: NEW ITALIAN-AMERICAN WRITING and she teaches poetry in Arcadia University's low-residency MFA program in Glenside, Pennsylvania.

Mykyta Ryzhykh lives in Ukraine and is winner of the international competition Art Against Drugs and Ukrainian contests Vytoky, Shoduarivska Altanka, Khortytsky dzvony; laureate of the literary competition named after Tyutyunnik, Lyceum, Twelve, named after Dragomoshchenko. Nominated for Pushcart Prize. Published many times in the journals *Dzvin, Dnipro, Bukovinian magazine, Polutona, Rechport, Topos, Articulation, Formaslov, Literature Factory, Literary Chernihiv, Tipton Poetry Journal, Stone Poetry Journal, Divot journal, dyst journal, Superpresent Magazine, Allegro Poetry Magazine, Alternate Route, Better Than Starbucks Poetry & Fiction Journal, Littoral Press, Book of Matches*, on the portals *Litcenter, Ice Floe Press* and *Soloneba*, in the Ukrainian literary newspaper.

Claire Scott is an award winning poet in Oakland, California who has received multiple Pushcart Prize nominations. Her work has been accepted by the *Atlanta Review, Bellevue Literary Review, New Ohio Review, Enizagam* and *Healing Muse* among others. Claire is the author of *Waiting to be Called* and *Until I Couldn't*. She is the co-author of *Unfolding in Light: A Sisters' Journey in Photography and Poetry*.

Tipton Poetry Journal

Mary Sexson lives in Indianapolis and is author of the award-winning book, *103 in the Light, Selected Poems 1996-2000* (Restoration Press), and co-author of *Company of Women, New and Selected Poems* (Chatter House Press). Her poetry has appeared in *Tipton Poetry Journal, Laureate, Hoosier Lit, Flying Island, New Verse News, Grasslands Review,* and *Last Stanza Poetry Journal,* among others. She has recent work in *Reflections on Little Eagle Creek, Anti-Heroin Chic,* and *Last Stanza Poetry Journa*l Issue #8. Finishing Line Press will publish her manuscript, *Her Addiction, An Empty Place at the Table,* in 2023. Sexson's poetry is part of the INverse Poetry Archives for Hoosier Poets.

Annette Sisson's poems appear in *Valparaiso Poetry Review, Birmingham Poetry Review, Rust+Moth, Lascaux Review, Glassworks,* and many others. Her first full-length book, *Small Fish in High Branches,* was published by Glass Lyre (2022), and her second is currently questing for a publisher. Her poems have placed in *Frontier New Voices, The Fish Anthology,* and a number of other contests, and several have been nominated for The Pushcart and Best of the Net. A native Hoosier, Annette now lives in Nashville, Tennessee.

Heidi Slettedahl is a US-UK dual national living in New York State who goes by a slightly different name professionally. She has been published in a variety of online literary journals and hopes to live up to her potential now that she is over 50.

Wally Swist's books include *Huang Po and the Dimensions of Love* (Southern Illinois University Press, 2012), selected by Yusef Komunyakaa as co-winner in the 2011 Crab Orchard Series Open Poetry Contest, and *A Bird Who Seems to Know Me: Poems Regarding Birds & Nature* (Ex Ophidia Press, 2019), the winner of the 2018 Ex Ophidia Press Poetry Prize. His recent poems have appeared in *Asymptote, Chicago Quarterly Review, Hunger Mountain: Vermont College of Fine Arts Journal, The Montreal Review, Pensive: A Global Journal of Spirituality and the Arts, Poetry London, Scoundrel Time, and The Seventh Quarry Poetry Magazine (Wales).* He lives in Massachusetts.

Jim Tilley lives in New York State and has published three full-length collections of poetry and a novel with Red Hen Press. His short memoir, *The Elegant Solution,* was published as a Ploughshares Solo. His poem, *On the Art of Patience,* was selected by Billy Collins to win Sycamore Review's Wabash Prize for Poetry. Four of his poems have been nominated for a Pushcart Prize. His next poetry collection, *Ripples in the Fabric of the Universe: New & Selected Poems,* will be published in June 2024.

Gene Twaronite is the author of four collections of poetry as well as the rhyming picture book *How to Eat Breakfast.* His first poetry book *Trash Picker on Mars,* published by Kelsay Books, was the winner of the 2017 New Mexico-Arizona Book Award for Arizona poetry. gene has an MA in education, and leads a poetry workshop for the University of Arizona OLLI program. A former New Englander, Gene now lives in Tucson. Follow more of his poetry at genetwaronite.poet.com

Since 2008, **Dana Yost** has published eight books with a ninth forthcoming from Finishing Line Press and has been nominated for three Pushcart Prizes and won the 2020 chapbook contest of the South Dakota State Poetry Society. Dana lives in Sioux Falls, South Dakota.

Editor

Barry Harris is editor of the *Tipton Poetry Journal* and several anthologies by Brick Street Poetry. He has published one poetry collection, *Something At The Center*.

Married and father of two grown sons, Barry lives in Brownsburg, Indiana and is retired from Eli Lilly and Company.

His poetry has appeared in *Kentucky Review, Valparaiso Poetry Review, Grey Sparrow, Silk Road Review, Saint Ann's Review, North Dakota Quarterly, Boston Literary Magazine, Night Train, Silver Birch Press, Flying Island, Awaken Consciousness, Writers' Bloc, Red-Headed Stepchild* and *Laureate: The Literary Journal of Arts for Lawrence*. One of his poems was on display at the National Museum of Sport and another is painted on a barn in Boone County, Indiana as part of Brick Street Poetry's Word Hunger public art project. His poems are also included in these anthologies: *From the Edge of the Prairie; Motif 3: All the Livelong Day;* and *Twin Muses: Art and Poetry*.

He graduated a long time ago with a major in English from Ball State University.

Made in United States
Orlando, FL
12 February 2024